NECTAR

NECTAR

C.L. BROWN

Shadow
Leaf

Nectar copyright © 2017 by Clifton L. Brown. All rights reserved. Printed in the United States of America by Shadow Leaf Press. This book may not be reproduced in whole or in part without written permission, except in the case of brief quotations embodied in critical articles and reviews; nor may any part of this book be reproduced, stored in a retrieval system or transmitted in any form by any means, electronic, mechanical, photocopying, recording or other without written permission of the publisher or author.

Published by Shadow Leaf Press

ISBN: 978-1-7350311-8-7

ATTENTION: SCHOOLS & BUSINESSES
Shadow Leaf Press' books are available at quantity discounts with bulk purchases for educational, business, or sales promotional use. For information, please email the publisher and author at: shadowleafpress@gmail.com

OTHER TITLES BY C.L. BROWN

Bare
Loud Whispers of Silent Souls
The Eyes That Swallowed the Midday Sun

Contents

Thanksgiving	xiii
Dedication	xv
Acknowledgments	xvii
Guide of Light	**xxiii**
Impartation	2
Still Worthy	4
Fellowship of Fear	7
Spoken Word	9
Servant	11
39	13
Nomad	15
Rebirth	17
All Things New	19
The Nature of Seeing	20
Redeemer	21
Forest of God	22
Guiding Light	24
Paradox	28

Omnipresence	29
Rest	31
Residence of Grace	33
Birth of Life	35
When the Voices End	36
Traveler	38
Life After	40
Aspirations of the Caged	42
Cornerstone	43
Way of Water	44
Chrysalis	**47**
Elegy for Yesterday	50
Chrysalis	53
Drifter	55
Domestic Conflict	57
Eyes for Me	59
Self-Expression	61
Away with Childish Things	64
Away From Me	68
Caged Freedom	71
Mockingbird	73

Stranger Among Friends … 75

Seed Time and Harvest … 77

As I AM … 79

Realization … 81

Dark of the Night … 83

Rain … 86

Weaver … 89

Empty … 91

Fool's Gold … 93

Journey's End … 95

For They Know Not What They Do … 98

Ambrosia … **105**

Gift … 108

Convergence … 112

The Musician and the Muse … 117

Cycles of Devotion … 119

Honey Making … 120

Therapy … 122

Daily Bread … 125

Heart-to-Heart … 127

Palace … 129

Bloom	133
Holy Ground	135
Watchman	137
Reflecting Pool	139
Mirage	141
Rain Dance	143
Replenished	144
Song of Her King	146
In Her Garden	148
Resurrecting Love	150
Guardians of Her Soul	152
Morning's Brew	154
Cello's Lament	155
Rainclouds and Sunflowers	157
Alchemy	159
Sweet Spell	161
God in Her Flesh	163
Awhile	166
Headdress	168
Stargazing	170
Arise	171

I Drink of You	173
Gardener	175
Voice of Silence	176
Healer	178
Addiction	180
Memoirs of Her King	182
Stranger in Her Skin	185
Reflection	186
Morning's Meditation	188
It Is Really You	191
Heart Song	192
I Search for You	193
You're Not That Amazing	195
In the Cool of Every Day	198
Between the Heavens and Myself	200
Sacred Seed	201
Wind Chimes	202
Benediction	203

Thanksgiving

Though my feet often stray, my heart remains faithful to the Light. I give all honor to the I AM. The One in whom I live and move and have my being.

Dedication

To my heart, Luna, I dedicate this book to you. As I write this, I sense a very tangible surge of love coursing through my entire being for you. I haven't seen you yet. I haven't touched you yet. I haven't heard the sound of your laughter. I am not familiar with your smile, nor the way your beautiful soul will try to hide behind your eyes, and yet, I know you will reveal the wellspring of my virgin love.

When your mom told me that I was going to be a father, I was both afraid and excited. I knew you would be the greatest part of me to date, but I wasn't quite sure how to process that. The days are passing now, and with them, the fear has found a place in the wind of love that has swept me over. All that remains now is the excitement of holding you, of kissing you. All that remains now is this sublime sentiment of love, and indescribable imaginations of me sweeping you off the ground as you run to me.

It is Thanksgiving Day today. It will be some time before you fully understand what this day truly means, but suffice it to say, it is a day that people allow awareness to fill their hearts as they think about those things that matter most. Well, today, you matter most. Your mom and I have so much to be thankful for, because you are nine weeks old, and growing so bravely inside her love.

I want you to know that, daily, I pray for you. I often place my hand over your mom's belly, and I pray for you. I ask God to immerse you in the purest love. I ask God for the strength, the courage, the love, the patience, and the wisdom to help me guide you into your light; into your purpose, into the greatest version of yourself.

I vow, as long as air is passing through my lungs, to be here for you. To love you. To guide you. To protect you. To support you. To wipe your tears when they leave your weakened eyes, and speak words to help the healing of your breaking heart. Already, in you, I have found my guiding light. The personification of my love. My purpose.

Your mom and I are anxiously waiting to welcome you into our world. Until then, I pray divine peace over you as you undergo this first of many amazing journeys to come. You are already a winner, my sweet baby girl. You are my winner. I love you with everything in me. See you at the finish line, my heart.

Acknowledgments

It is literally impossible for me to name every single person who has inspired and encouraged me on this path. I, simply, do not know all of your names, but you purchased this book at the recommendation of a friend. You've gifted one of my books to a friend. You've commented on a social media post. You've sat in an audience, and allowed me to share my heart with you. You've shaken my hand. You've hugged me. You've told me that something of all that I have said or written has inspired you to do, and be better. You've been vulnerable, and you've trusted me enough to share your heart with me. You live in Nigeria. You've inspired me from Jamaica. You've messaged me from Trinidad and Tobago. You've encouraged me from Venezuela. You've shared my story in Holland. You've posted a beautiful review from Canada. You've asked me to come share my gift with you in Ethiopia. You've attended my book signings in the United States. You share my vision. You support my passion. You are such an amazing gift to me, and I am so thankful for you. What I have done with this gift I could not have done without you. I am eternally grateful.

To the following people, I thank you from the core of my being. My beautiful mother, Hyacinth Brown. Mom, I will love you forever. You were my rock. You are my rock. Thank you for raising me to be the man that I am. My father, Earl. Thank you for having the courage to be a strong foundation. My siblings: Patricia, Michelle, Pamela, Ortnell, Jermaine, and Keron. Thank you, guys, for the love and support. My friends: Chris, Keisha, Duane, Leon, Roan, Nicola, Michelle, Tanya, Elena, Carlos, Jon, Debbie, Jason, Marlon, Vanessa, Lesley-Ann, Joy, Ron, and Fallon. I thank each, and every one of you for being a "cup of water" when I needed a drink.

A special thanks to my best friend, life partner, lover, and the mother of my child, Crystal-Ann. Baby, you have been the embodiment of God's love. Thank you for being you. Thank you for encouraging and empowering me every single day. Thank you for loving me. Thank you for allowing me to share the sacredness of your being. It is my philosophy that love is the art of servants, and that the true heart of God hides in the souls of those who serve selflessly. You serve me selflessly every single time the sun rises and while it remains in the sky. You serve me every single time the moon rises and while it remains in the sky. Thank you from the depths of me, my love.

Dr. Dan Graffeo, you continue to inspire me. Whenever I need to go below the surface, you are always a wiling companion. Thank you for your words of wisdom, and enlightenment. Thank you for our soul-enriching conversations. You are truly a godsend.

But then I happened
upon the redolence
of your nectar
And the innocence
of my love
You shackled
in unrequited surrender

Guide of Light

*If you wish to know God,
get to know **love**.*

*If you wish to know love,
get to know the **heart of a servant**.*

*If you wish to know the heart of a servant,
serve.*

Impartation

Should you close your heart to the misunderstandings
of they which slumber in the teachings of love,
there is something ethereally beautiful
about a flower exhaling her last breath.

For when she no longer wore the captivity of the soul,
and the heavens reclaimed the aroma of God,
I was smitten reading the letters time composed
into her moldering petals.

I felt divine compassion streaming from both eyes
as I stood shedding pieces of her
no one's ever seen.

She gifted my heart the use of the pen
—in return—
inhaling her last breath in the labor of my fingers
engraving her essence into the soul of this poem,
I gifted her wings freedom's direction.

I wrote—unrelenting—
mining her, like priceless minerals,
from compressed imaginations.

And so, she gave color to my musings.
Embellishing my achromatic existence.

And I gave praise.

For when she'd extricated herself
from the snare of limited understanding,
—redeeming my irredeemable—
I saw God in the petals of a flower
imparting to me the sacred teachings of love.

And I gave praise.

You are bothered at the sound of the water's drip because you do not know the weight of the thirst that I carry.

Still Worthy

With no eyes, I saw God.
She was there,
dancing with the spirits of Sufi poems,
extrapolating the visible from the invisible.

She moved with a kind of grace
I in all my learnings could never shroud
in meaningful words.

I watched her wading in the poetry of all the universes
where the seen and the unseen,
the heard and the unheard,
the felt and the unfelt,
eventually converge.

I said to God.
Great God!
You have fashioned such marvelous wonders.
The colors of all the oceans
and how they embody the souls
of drifting skies.

You allow the highest of mountains
to rise up from the lowest of valleys
in the balancing of the wise and the fool.

You made sound outside the reach of an ear
and yet the sound
—like you—
is a master soother of the most troubled among souls.

You cause stars to encircle stars,
and in the intimate dance of their burning flames,
the butterfly places its wings in the invisible mystery
that takes life to my flesh.

You cause the transcending leaf
to rest in the cradle of the river's rage,
and the mind in passing to become entirely still

God, I said, you are great!
You are the storehouse of all things.
The known and the unknown.

At such knowledge,
my soul within ceases never to ascribe to you great praise.

But tell me, God.
Why then did you think to fashion something
as unworthy as I?

I who have so little,
and what little I do possess,
in selfishness,
I endow myself every single chance that I get.

God replied,
"My beloved son,
the deaf man listens
to the Nightingale's song in vain,
and the blind man's gaze upon the stars at night
is the origin of immense frustration.
But he that finds the stars in his own eyes,
and he that hears the Nightingale's song
in his own heart,
he has danced with his God
in the presence of all the universes
veiled within him."

If you aren't prepared to receive it, stop asking for it. It is a fool who prays for the rain without first preparing a container to catch water.

Fellowship of Fear

He said, if Love is a leaf,
God is its shape,
its veins,
and the pigment it was gifted of the rainbow's kindness.

We passed time inside the decadent abstractions
of his mind.

But in his fellowship,
it was fear I felt most as contempt seeped through
the porous musings of this object of sin.

He tried separating my soul from its flesh
in his quest to serve that brutish self.

He served that brutish self.

I am now free.

He said if God is a leaf,
Love is its shape,
its veins,
and the pigment it was gifted of the rainbow's kindness.

And so, he was with Love
but became the playground of fear
as he plucked his God from the stem that sustained him.

Such ignorance.

I watched Love falling from his care to the place
passing souls find the pathway to life,
and so learned, there is no light to illuminate the eyes
of the heart that isn't willing to survey beyond itself.

When you finally open your eyes, you will realize that stars do not try to outshine other stars. They simply shine. Yes, some more brilliantly than others, but it is collectively that they manifest the glory of the darkness, the progenitor of light. You see, the darkness is to the light what the ocean is to the wave. The latter does not exist without the former, and the former is dead without the latter. But truly, there is no latter, and truly there is no former. There is only the one. Stars shine because darkness is perceptible. You shine because I am perceptible. Your attempt to undo me, then, is truly an attempt to undo yourself.
For you are, because I AM.

Spoken Word

Inside the place where our voice is one
Where my total self speaks in silence

I perceived that imperceptible one
The one called by untold names
The Unknown

I was anchored in the soul of our foremost mother,
imbibing her love as a new born cleaved to the breast,
taking life of her life

Chanting songs of redemption
that found inception in that place
that once fermented my fear,
I broke free as peace cascaded
from the guardians of my soul
to the washing of my feet

"Una palabra de la boca de Dios",
whispered the Sacred Blackness
as the tumultuous sea of my mind
found peace at the command of His tongue

Thus, silent whispers bestowed I
on the messenger passing in the trees
both day and night

The one eulogizing for the rising
of the fallen Son

Una palabra,
Redeemer.

As a child, I sowed seeds, but then—as befitting a child—I would rise early the next morning to uncover them—the eagerness of my unseasoned self seeking unseasonal growth. I thank God that childhood was only a season. A necessary season, but a season nonetheless. For now I have learned to trust the process.

Servant

Look at Love
Ever yielding

She is a servant of servants
Ever yielding

She is a teacher of wonderful things
Ever yielding

What burdens can you cast upon her
that she hasn't already toted?

What wrong can keep you from the depths
of forgiveness that she calls her bosom?

She has been kissed with deceitful lips,
and yet death drinks of her cup at the offense
of her deceiver

When all else have taken arms against you,
her hands bear scented flowers
of the sweetest compassion

For she understands that a stone casted in fear
is not a rod of correction

Her only recourse then is to take onto herself
all of your encumbrances

Ever yielding

Not until I was sick. Not until circumstances feasted on my aspirations, did I know the mercies of Healing. At my bedside, she unfolded her soul, and I freely took what I did not deserve.

39

Thirty-nine years searching
This morning
I saw God
Sitting in the muted rays
Of the infant sun

Meditating

I sat there with Him
Along the edge of a tiny pond
Whispering tranquil things
Between a thicket
Of silence

For the first time
In all my days,
I knew the weight
Of the Unoccupied mind

God and me
And uncounted time

I am weary of those who claim to love God, yet the only thing in this world that they truly value, is human life. As if the God who created the man isn't the same God who created the elephant, and the ant.

Nomad

Like a chick's feather
surrendering its will
to the dicey wind,
my heart moves
with such mindful bliss
through paths
it hasn't paved.

But for the mind,
that tenacious seeker of truth,
there is no harness.

How then can the two walk
when their journeys aren't one?

Seeking light
in the company of darkness,
I stand a conflicted man.

Roaming the night
a disembodied light.

My vagrant feet
sauntering the pavements
of dimly lit streets.

The deeper that I descend into God the more aware I am that barely anything is in my control, and that is OK. But here is the beautiful part, I have learned that the tiny bit that I do control is as needed as the whole lot that I do not. Beyond that, I am now aware of the fact that all of it, the parts that I control, and the parts that I do not control, are all working together to manifest the very best of me, the very best for me, the very best for our world.

Rebirth

When the darkness finally engulfed me
amidst the light, and balance manifested itself
like a flower that weathered the night
to greet the first dawn of new beginnings,
I asked of Him that is forever.

I laid my soul bare,
finding the courage to inquire
from the root of my being.

While the words were yet taking shape
within my soul as the newly conceived
in the womb of Love,
His still small voice permeated my silence.

And there,
in the divine softness of Love,
I was compelled to be true unto myself.

And thus,
freedom was given the freedom t
o break the bonds that held me captive.

And thus,
my truth is a tapped well in the place
I've laid in prior days—amidst the lies
that blanketed my truth as the sands
of the great desert.

That dried-up blade of grass and I came under the lashing of the same gust of wind. Only, it danced, while I sat with silence, watching. We were both praising the one God from two beautifully contrasting perspectives.

All Things New

I woke up ablaze in your fire—
watching my former self giving way
to the better me lying in your gracious hands.

I was a captive of the sight of love molding fear.
There you were exfoliating aged weakness
while embers of the old me
took to the cold midnight air.

Repeatedly,
you extinguished and ignited me
like a master sculptor
giving purpose to useless iron.

I no longer have thoughts of the days
that are not acquainted with you.

Former, present, nor future.

You are the expanse of everything I could ever be.
And so, my soul moves through you unbothered.
And like a trouble-less man in tranquil slumber.

Yet I am awake,
enlightened,
evolving.

The Nature of Seeing

I was taught to shun the darkness
I was taught to revere the light

And yet, without the death of the sun,
I would've never beheld
the glory of the heavens

Redeemer

You are not of this place
Your roots have no place inside this ground

Before you descended,
your were light interweaved between stars,
tracing the perimeter of the ether

Having never taken a sip of the rain's offering,
you've blossomed in the air of my immensely arid heart

You are the sweet-scented flower whose nectar
beckons for the creatures of God's garden

They come running by day
By night you set free your irresistible scent,
guiding the feet of the eyes the darkness has subdued

You are a source of strength
for all who have set their lips to drink of you
As a bridge hanging, you are the sure way
between the heavens and myself

When I needed a place in the Light of God,
I disrobed myself of words
I've purposely cocooned myself in,
silencing my soul in the audience
of your grand symphony

Standing like the majesty of a tree
between the unforgiving sun
and my fragile skin,
officiating my sentencing,
you deliver a judgment of sweet compassion

Forest of God

Take me to the forest of God
Where the risen sun makes of gold
The spires of souls rooted in the grace of the earth
Where time sits in awe of the works of her own hands
Prolonging the elation of youthful hearts

There I sat once in reach of Spirit's song
Enthralled by the euphoric anecdotes
of a glad-hearted flute

When the moon shies away from her brilliance, pray for the light. When the sun is depleted of mercy, pray for the shade. But when the sun lies gasping for air, and his moon makes her way to the birthing canal, bask yourself in the glory of this balance, for your cycle of salvation is once again upon you.

Guiding Light

So many roads to choose from
How does one find the destination
when the path is a web of confusion
leading away from the self
only to come back again?

So many signs pointing, redirecting
He's making circles around himself again

The Son rises in his eye,
still blindness blankets his direction
Rending the veil of his religion
He's looking within

Can he see the sun in the absence of its light?

The voice of repentance reverberating inside the hollow
of his hallowed self

Moving towards your voice's clear distinction
He runs to you with fear-shackled feet
Falling
Rising

The heaviness of his burdens clanging
like steel chains against the hardened road
he's paved within his fruitless mind

He finds peace when the world sleeps
Lying weak,
partially covered beneath
blood-stained sheets
atoning for himself

For though you know every inch of him,
still, he's ashamed of the truth in his nakedness

So many questions
So many answers
So many faces of truth
Lies disguised multiply like parasites
feasting on his formless void

But the flowers reflect your face
So, he waters the thorn bushes drawing his blood

The rainbow recites the song of Grace
So, he stands hands raised,
wounds to the rain,
washing away the lifeblood
of his former selves

The homeless man's needs
in the place his lack is abundant
manifests his divinity,
his humanity
Because for the King to ascend,
he must submit to the heart of the servant

But the preacher man pollutes his truth,
convincing him to wash the dirt off the hands
he used to sow mustard seeds

But though hope has no eyes, it sees all things

I saw you once in my disobedience
while I gave my undivided self to myself
Would I have seen you still had I followed
the signs you'd given?

The rebel's ways led thousands to you
Should I place my quailing feet in the steps he left,
will I rise in the glory of his death?

Betrayal is served on the platters of friends' lips
False accusations

Mindless manipulations
My ambition nailed to the idle words
crossing between them

You see, when conformity knew fear
She conceived
But I was aborted
So, though the road narrows
where fear becomes good company
in the absence of courage,
I am still here
Still confused
Still afraid
But still walking towards the clear distinction
of your loving voice

When you seek happiness, do not put a face to it. Do not put a name, nor a sensation. Allow it to be what it needs be, what it must be. Keep no agendas. Keep no expectations. Do not seek it in garments of familiarity, for the wolf in sheep's clothing still carries sharp fangs.

Paradox

The darkness that incited
the most intense sense
of fear within me
is the same darkness
that propelled me
into the supernal embrace of light
I lost myself to here
That is how I found my way

Omnipresence

Of the One that is,
yet is not,
I asked,
gift me the sight of your face

Then the peacock engrossed the heart of his beloved
Unveiling the masterpiece painted beneath his wings

Of the One that is,
yet is not,
I asked,
gift me the joy your heart

Then I beheld as a man having no possessions,
a vagabond,
gave of his last meal
to a bird having both wings

I smiled
Then I gave praise

Time is a woman to be courted. The wise knows she will deliver in the arms of patience.

Rest

I emptied myself into the deep of the sea
I was tired of running
Running for what seemed days innumerable
Running as the sun fell from the aging sky
Running until the stars no longer lit the way of hope

Along the way I lost a bit of myself,
but I never relented making strides
towards the depths of the waiting sea

When I found what little that remained of me,
standing there at her shoreline,
I saw a wrinkled leaf,
bearing the hue of my skin,
falling from Heaven

I watched how with grace it rode the unseen wind
Falling from Grace
I watched how it fell in the embrace
of the waiting sand
I watched the sea washing my feet
as she sang praises over the aging man
that had returned from troubles sought

I beheld the moment her careful waves
took that fallen leaf away from me

That leaf that fell from Grace

I emptied myself into the deep of the sea
Like a leaf,
I was no longer running
I was no longer

All praises

I have opened to you the entirety of my truth, but you feed on foolish things as a cow lying in the meadow at night—regurgitating and feasting on old things amidst the abundance of the new.

Residence of Grace

It was not in the heavens
For countless nights I laid against the earth
gazing into them

It was not in the Daffodil's dancing
as she took turns waltzing between the wind
and the mild midday rain

You see, I gazed until the song had ended,
and her petals were nestled in the compassion
of the earth

It was not in the symphony of many instruments
For I listened with the fullness of my heart
Yet, still, my grief could not be consoled

It was in the quiet whispers
of a baby's tiny fingers crawling gently against my skin
that I found the place
God truly dwells

It was in your water my soul transcended. The quiet serenade of the tranquil sea. What sweet lullaby of rainbow-washed clouds beneath the crystalline depths of Grace. Your wind has unearthed the secrets of my deep. Mountains of fear plunging to sweet death. The heavenly chorus of perpetual waves harmonizing while salvation sings as an impassioned Night Songstress.
I was.
I AM.

Birth of Life

I am the mist
that brings due the morning's due
I am the awakening of the Hibiscus' petals

I lay eyes to the womb
of the absence of myself
Watching as she holds to life
Carrying hope as a mother
imbued with the life-giving light
of her own darkness

What you seek is emptiness
outside the nature of love

Your heart,
in the fellowship of my ethereal self,
gallops wildly beneath your breast
as untamed beasts of unending fields
where freedom is snared in the breath
binding the living soul to dying flesh

Exhale!
Walk where courage is obsolete
Where fear is non-existing
Where death submits to life
like a servant upon bended knees
in the presence of the Great King

When the Voices End

I was drowning in the deep of voices
I was unfamiliar with
Bobbing between life and death
atop waves of untainted sadness
while a tattered guitar
harmonized the laying bare
of my soul on crumpled sheets
of scribbled-on paper

Have you ever tried to undo
what has been etched into the
unyielding memory of time?

I have

But the things the past has written
cannot simply be unwritten
And all efforts to mask them just leaves
a bigger mess that you weren't fully prepared to deal with

But the eventual outcome of all the voices is silence

And it is in this state of being
that you will hear the only voice
that truly matters

I quieted my mind
Now it speaks

If you wish to feed a man, do not chase him down. For in so doing, he will flee in terror. Rather, be still, and allow your fruits to manifest. At such a time, if he craves what you are, he will find his way to your table.

Traveler

I am a traveler
Eagerly exploring the inner parts
and the outer parts of you

In anticipation of my sojourning
within the walls of your love,
my soul perused the books they've written of you

But now,
being here,
I see clearly the misperceptions
that prematurely severed my infancy
from the womb that sustained me

Still, I carry on

Some days the terrain of faith seem impassable
These boulders of egos standing boldly ahead of me
Dust clouds of doubt
Unanswered prayers my mind keeps
resurrecting from the ground
though I've repeatedly recited eulogies over them

But though fear is a loyal companion,
I often wander alone to the darker regions of your peace
Places his feet will not permit him to venture

And when I'm there,
there aren't colors that I do not see
Nor forms that I do not take
Nor textures that I do not feel

And so, expressions of the inner-self
I transcribe,
—like cave writings—
inside the inner chambers of your grace

For in giving me passage to and from
your most holy of places,
I have learned that you encompass the heights
and the depths of all that I am
And am not

So, I go again
I come again
You are never the same
Yet my steps are never uncertain
Nor my soul bewildered

And so, I am a traveler
Eagerly exploring the inner parts,
and the outer parts of you

Life After

In absolute humility,
mother stood boldly
before the reach of death

Her soul was answering the call
no one can turn away from

But with courage in her eyes,
"Do not allow anyone to tell you whether
you are going to Heaven or Hell", she said
"Because I am dying, and I do not know
where I am going"

Truth is not eyes rummaging through the darkness. It doesn't seek. It is a light perched atop a high hill. It is sought after.

Aspirations of the Caged

When companionship you find
lying with misunderstanding,
I too partake of this infidelity

The outcast of conformity,
it is my destiny to leave behind
all treasures of familiarity

And though arrayed in garments
my hands have never removed,
home abundantly awaits

Why does the wild-born covet fences of fear?
Walls of doubt?
Why does the rolling stone find a home
where its heart will never settle?

Fear is a seed of the inhibited mind
And the gardener of truth
knows the precious nature of water

What is now shall not always be
What keys you hold shall one day not posses any doors
Do not make of time a compliant fool

Cornerstone

Though I was conceived in the blank slate
of infinite possibility,
there are no eyes for me

Such busy,
beautiful,
bold wrinkles burning through
sundry shades of coveted brown

Your sun has seen me through the progression
of the days the clouds forgot to stay

Your eyes,
without effort,
washed over abstractions of love
like water-infused colors over textured paper

This was the hour of my birthing

I am now rising through the perspectives
of infinite possibility
Watching your intentions manifesting
the personification of purpose

I am coming together,
exactly how you see fit

Way of Water

Take me into you
Immerse me
Deeply
Let me breathe you in
Birth me again and again
until my end finds again
the place it all began

For though my vessel bears blemishes,
and my water has known the lips of unclean spirits,
still, I am able bear the burden of the thirsty

So, take me into you
Immerse me
Deeply
Let me breathe you in
Birth me again and again
until my heart finds again
the place we both began

Chrysalis

Perhaps God is, as I AM, a tormented soul finding solace within itself.

Elegy for Yesterday

On this day, change has come

I am delivered with the birthing of the morning
For the night is a womb and a place of restoration

I was once among the broken
A casualty of the battle Yesterday waged with Tomorrow
Attempting to inhibit the harvest of Grace

But when the transcended Sun inseminated the dawn,
I rose the first fruit of the Universe's knowing
the flesh of Man

Drinking of the Mountain's provision
while the ghosts of defeated dreams retreat in shame,
I pour libations listening to the elegy
God recited in honor of Yesterday

But once, while wandering outside His Light,
I saw how misplaced dreams eventually
become victims of the night

My aching heart roared like thunder
Mourning as thoughts like earth-kissing lightning
fell to that lower self I sought freedom from

I saw how the dust of dying stars gave shape
to the form that shrouds my eternal being

I saw how the lips of Eternity's love
fell gracefully between my eyes
Giving sight to the man that kept me from
my truest version

I now stand the manifestation of my truest self
God walking again among men

Because Last Night conceived Today
in the ashes of Yesterday
Giving birth to the one whose wings took
to the brilliant skies to play

So, rise I will as my Father did
For the night is the womb of restoration
And a place for the fallen who seek redemption

I AM nothing more than you make of me.
I AM nothing less than you make of yourself.

Chrysalis

I am rising now
I won't be much longer with you
You will see me again
Just not as you are

The gate to life leads within, friend
But only the brave at heart
There the fearful have no place

I have lived,
but it was in death
that I found the remains of my life

I am rising now
I won't be much longer with you

Do you not see pieces of the fractured me
falling to the ocean where life and death finally converge?

I am only ahead, friend
I will see you again
Just not as you are

While with you,
I composed what I often did not comprehend
But God gave unction
And my heart, though broken, was willing

This is my benediction
My chrysalis has broken
I am rising now
Falling to the ocean where life and death finally converge

Some days my thoughts evolve into uncaged butterflies. Other days they are fire-breathing dragons, trapped, trying to burn their way out of my soul.

Drifter

Fear is a fire bearing the colors of dense clouds
when dying suns bestow their last bit of light
in defiance of coming night

Like a winged serpent, I've spewed it from my own lips
And I've watched my own flesh and my own bones
become utterly consumed

I was told for him to find God,
man must first pass through his flame
And so, through this self-inflected destruction,
I, in fact, am searching

I am searching the lies they've fed me
Seeking a truth I am not acquainted with

I have prayed
I have quieted my soul
I have listened

I have searched the ritual dance of rooted trees
under the love-spell of the night's breeze
I have searched the words of conviction piercing
the lying lips of deceitful preacher men

I have searched
But I have not seen God
But I have not heard God
But I have not felt God
For I have not seen myself
For I have not heard myself
For I have not felt the air in my lungs
that bridges me to all things eternal

And thus, I am a drifter
A fool seeking life in the realm of the dead

I am love, expressed.

Domestic Conflict

Alone in the conquest of darkness
toiled this poem in the deep of my weakness

Twisting and turning
No comfort she found

Feeling her way through the crippling pain
I could no longer retain

Her weakened eyes
wading through crested waves
of my grieving soul

The cold hands of confusion
fastened about her determination
Devoid of conscious volition,
she moves within the strangeness of myself

But the thoughtful moon gifted her light,
and hope encircled me as a great herd encircles
the defenseless calf

Feeling her way through the unanswered questions
my soul could no longer contain

Her weakened eyes
wading through crested waves
of my darkness

Entirely useless

*How gracious this grand illusion
allowing every man his fair dose of insanity.*

Eyes for Me

I let go
of me
of you
of hurt
of hurting
of being loved
of loving
of being seen
of seeing
of speaking
of listening
of needing to understand
of needing to be understood

Like the sun rising
where it has never fallen

I come back to the place
I was never away from

Illusions fading like unheard whispers nestled
in the passing wind

I am learning and unlearning me

Delusions of God

There is no need to find love. It is not lost. Simply become aware that you are love, expressed. Then, consciously begin expressing yourself a little more each day.

Self-Expression

Can you separate love from itself?
Beauty?
Truth?
Compassion?
Strength?

Can these things be divided?
Can they be separated?

Is love not complete in,
and inseparable from itself?
Beauty?
Truth?
Compassion?
Strength?

Can love procreate fear?
Truth lies?
Beauty ugliness?
Strength weakness?
Compassion indifference?

God!
Can God be separated from itself?

You see, I have traveled the expanse of myself
I have sojourned within the depths of myself
I have met me, face to face, and I was in awe of myself
And I have learned there is no work in my hands
to earn the love of Love

For I am Love, expressed

When the ocean's water satiates its curiosity
of lurking sand, is the water among the sand
separate from the ocean?

Is not the water among the sand the ocean, expressed?

See, it is I who hold the key to self-acceptance
And so,
by God's grace,
in the presence of great adversity,
when the light in the eyes of hope grew dimmed,
and the path ahead seemed uncertain,
I reached for the light within,
and so learned that I am sufficient

So, you see!
I AM beautiful
I AM truth
I AM compassion
I AM strength
I AM Love, expressed

You cannot divide me even as you cannot divide Light
Truth
Compassion
Beauty
Strength
God

For I AM all these things,
expressed

The needs of the seed are not the needs of the blossoming tree. This is why bees don't buzz around them. If your associations are not changing as you grow, you will never bear your fruit.

Away with Childish Things

You didn't believe in me
But I hold no resentments

You flourished in my dry season
Drinking from the cup selfishness
held to your satiated lips

You mocked the struggle of my roots
as they burrowed through doubt
trying to find the aquifer of confidence

Then when the winds came
passing violently through my leaves
and I was left with naked branches,
you sought the shade of other trees

But God showed mercy when the sun fell
after siphoning the needed waters
my wearied roots pulled from
the unforgiving deep

But God showed mercy
replenishing my need beneath the veil of blackness
while the moon kept me company

All through the night,
I fought hell and its demons
Reaching for the hand you never stretched out

But, I have beaten the odds

I have survived the strength of the day
and the might of the night
But God did they pound against me

Now, I stand rooted in the sea of confidence

Now, my fruit hangs from branches of strength
Now, you have come to replenish your strength

But, go ahead!
Go ahead!
Take from me!

Have your fill that life should keep you company

For though you didn't believe in me,
I hold no resentments

Noah was given specific dimensions for the Ark because it was never meant for him to save everything from his past. We often speak of how much we are moving to new dimensions in God, yet our arks do not have any walls. It is imperative that you understand that the instructions you were given were not accessories for the boat, but rather necessities for the float.

The dove doesn't teach her chick how to fly until its wings are able to sustain it, and the wise cannot impart truth until the heart is ready to receive it.

Away From Me

Empty
Hollowed
You were the space I wasted days
Watching my rise to fall
Much like the light that once
resided in your eyes

You were the nights gifting moons
that captivated my wide-eyed heart
while laden clouds shed grief
upon my sorrows

You resounded my frustrations
Indoctrinating me into the foolish ways of myself

I was the liberated fool imprisoned by your ignorance
The clown amused by your madness

The aroma of seagulls chirping
in the lullabies of the ocean I never heard,
how beautifully you sung me to sleep
while nightmares ushered my soul
into the darkest trenches of your mind

You were home in all its broken glory

In you, I've witnessed nights becoming mornings
Mornings becoming nights
Life and death mirroring each other
through our ambient existence
while we searched for one another
in the void of each other's eyes

Your answers took purpose to my questions
My questions you abandoned
in the frigid temperatures of your ego

As I watched myself succumbing to you,
I learned insanity indeed had a face

The puppet is truly his own master
The voice he moves to sans reluctance,
pulling those strings,
animating his own misery

My head often breaks covenant with my feet
permitting my eyes one more glance back
Because I am still salty

Sometimes the scent rising from your ash
causes my soul to crave just a taste
of the dearth I suffered with you

But I've retired myself from conjugal visits with conformity

I AM, after all
A new creation

The butterfly that broke free from your pupa

Like the earth, we all go through seasons. Right now, however, you and I are not suffering the same one. So, please, do not allow your snow clouds to stifle my sunshine.

Caged Freedom

A little bird alighted once
between my shade of aspirations,
and the blistering heat of defeated ambitions

I was her delight it seemed
as she sang to the heart of ebbing dreams

She could have flown wherever she wished,
but she sat amidst my solitude
serenading my sadness wonderfully with her gracious tune

Her song was the sound of soul-deep burdens
finding rest on the path freedom paved
while Chopin played preludes
at the commencement of brighter days

She had me feeling things I have never felt
Seeing things I have never seen
Hearing things I have never heard

She released me!

I was wide awake
Sleeping
Dreaming
Recalling my teaching

But I forsook my position
Lowering her into my possession
Imprisoning, again, my newly found freedom

One day, someone will be brave enough to rummage through the hurt, and the pain you wear so proudly in those defeated eyes. They will see the mess those before them left, and they will love you just the way you are. Not because they think you deserve it, but because they know that they do.

Mockingbird

I am a mockingbird
Echoing melodies my sadness never sung
Like falling suns serenading moonless nights
Like sad hearts cowering behind brilliant eyes
My song is my disguise

For your bewilderment, I sing
Masking my masterpiece of pain
I am the whispers of spring mornings
Though my soul shivers in the dead of winter

I am a mockingbird
The echoes of melodies my madness has never sung

In hunting for my life, my enemy has taught me that there is still something inside of me some would kill to have. I give thanks.

Stranger Among Friends

I've worn a thousand faces,
and I've stood in the midst of all these places
trying to find which of these identical strangers
I resembled most

But, I have learned,
all versions of Truth are, in fact, mistruths

All these faces resembling me,
and I was not found in any of them

So, I ran away
Formless
Colorless
Nameless
Without certain identify

I ran until I found The Potter
He passed me through His fire
Remastering my resemblance
to these identical strangers

He gave me shape
He gave me color
He showed me the one face
of all these strangers

And o!
How beautiful I AM in all my expressions

The ego will lament for water in the midst of all the oceans.

Seed Time and Harvest

I have opened my hands
Someone has taken from them

Knees to the ground,
I have raised my emptied cup
Someone has filled me up

How blessed I am among us vagabonds
that love should prepare for me a room
in her light to weather this night

I have spent days that fueled the jealousy of nights
in the noise of my darkened mind

With quieted lips,
my soul has weathered thoughts that nearly drowned me

I do not have the years ahead of me
to count the days behind me
that words snuck out of my soul
pleading my cause to God

They are still pleading

But this night, I will weather the darkness inside the light

For I heard once how God,
in his infinite existence,
reached deeply within Himself,
and pulled something of Himself
He Himself was unfamiliar with

So, may this night I finally embody the image
and the likeness of His infinite existence
as my hands lay open,
receiving all that I have given

*How is it you wish to be as free as the butterfly,
yet you fear your cocoon of solitude?*

As I AM

Sitting in the congregation of nature
like sinners in church pews
bearing big city blues

Warm tears cascading
down my darkened skin

The wind singing praises to the King
while the Sun baptizes me in the sermons
of songbirds under the holy anointing

Is this is not redemption?

My scars are signposts to wisdom. I will not hide behind them. I will wear them proudly, for they are the badges of the obstacles that failed to destroy me.

Realization

In my awakened state,
I collapsed into a dream
It was I alone
Not whiteness
Not blackness
Not another soul
Nor the scent of another's flesh

Just pure nothingness

Then a voice,
not resembling my own,
spoke clearly as my dust settled
in its aftermath of silence

"Count your blessings," it said
I AM nothing, I said
"Count your blessings," it said
I AM nothing, I said
"Count your blessings," it said
I AM nothing, I said

You have to believe in your light. You must! You must believe that your light is more than able to overcome any darkness. If you allow yourself to get to the place where this belief is as real to you as the air that you breathe, you'll suddenly realize that your mission is not to rid the world of darkness but rather to fill the world with light. For if you pour enough light into the world, the light will do what it does best, and the world will shine because of it.

Dark of the Night

Go with peace into the dark of the night

But be not dismayed
The lion's roar is but an echo hinged
on the vestiges of what time he was given

Last words I leave not with you
For when the sun's rise lies before you
like a carpet fit for the feet of noble men,
my lips shall speak of divine things
as my heart recounts the many days and ways
in which it has loved you

So, do not set your eyes on the light of the past,
for there is much to behold in the dark of this night

Go with peace into the dark of the night

Be not dismayed
The lion's roar is but an echo hinged
on the vestiges of what time he was given

I desired to dance with the wind. So, I toyed with the debris it was carrying. Then it changed direction, and I was left trying to collect the pieces of trash that captivated my misguided heart.

I am most intrigued by the spirit of solitude. Being a counselor, it listens to me. Being a scholar, it searches me. Being a master, it teaches me. Being a gentleman, it courted me when my desire to be loved transcended my submissiveness to fear.

Rain

O rain,
how meticulously you fall
against my naked skin,
as if to say,
I am here,
are you listening?

O rain,
how peacefully you sing over me
in the gloom of the morning,
as if to say,
I am here,
are you listening?

I am listening, rain
Listening with my whole heart

Do you know every droplet
that you bless me with
has a voice that is heard
among all other voices?

I am listening
Listening to the riches of the melodies you sing
How they fall upon my skin
as you permeate deeply within
infinite expressions of myself

Do you know every droplet
that you bless me with
has a voice that is heard
among all other voices?

I am listening, rain
Listening with my whole heart

I swam the length and the breadth of the ocean seeking water. Such absurdity—Searching the universe for an omnipresent God. Searching the presence of a woman for love. Walking these empty roads only to come back to myself again.

*There is something quite revealing in being rejected, refused, passed up. You see, God uses the foolishness of men to confound the wisdom of men. To feel rejected is indicative of the fact that you believe that you are worth something. Keep believing! Do not allow the blindness of men to rob you of the vision of God. You were rejected by men because God erected you above them. When they fight their battles to acquire their thrones, it is you who will be the Crown Jewel seated in the position they revere most.
So, be still.*

Weaver

The weaver weaves its web
By day
By night

In darkness
In light

Whether mighty storms move gentle skies
Or gentle breeze command the quietude of lifeless trees

Through and through
Where there are no eyes found
The weaver weaves its web
My pride to confound

Many birds eat seeds, but all seed-eating birds don't feed from the same tree. What you are isn't for everyone. So, never try to convince anyone that you are what they need. Be what you are without reservation, and those that desire what you are will always find themselves a seat at your table.

Empty

I poured you the last cup of me
You emptied it into the ground

Now you are thirsty
And lurking around the well of dust
I have become

In the morning, the sun against the skin is a welcoming reminder and reason for praise. At midday, he is loathed because he tries, by a great fire, all that passes through his watchful eye. But when evening comes, he is once again an object of adoration, only some who adore him are unaware they are ascribing praise to a dying man.

Fool's Gold

I have traveled a long and difficult journey
Stopping for meat at the empty tables
of idle women

Yet there is a place I was without lack
A place my queen sat in waiting
Longing to place my cold heart
against the warmth of her skin

Longing to replenish my flesh
if it means emptying her soul

But, I knew my fill in barren places
as idiocy guided my feet in the ways
my heart knew only pain

Searching for the home I left behind,
I became a madman
A vagabond

Now my queen sits at the right hand
of a strange King

Ruling the fruitful Kingdom
I have forsaken

In this life, the greatest day you will ever face is the day you realize that you are the sum of the mountains you've been speaking to, and make a conscious decision to begin speaking to yourself.

Journey's End

I was entrusted this mystery
The untold story of the young boy
tracking fading footsteps in the hardening mud

When the sun,
at the summit of the sky,
grew fiercely angry,
the mud,
in awe,
became deeply silent

The haziness of the boy's thoughts,
like heavy clouds,
rained on the fear already pooled
deeply within him

But his soul was merciful
So, his eyes flooded the mud that laid beneath him

And the mud,
once again,
began softly speaking

And so, the young boy,
unceasingly tracking steps he hasn't taken,
searching for a divine God
in his temporal existence,
finally caught sight of the genesis of life
that long took residence inside his juvenile heart

Remember, in sleep, the shepherd is roofed by the same heavens and nestled by the same earth as the sheep.

If you leave your door open, flies will enter your house. Before you begin to swat them, close your door. Otherwise, you might find yourself trapped in a perpetual habit of fruitless endeavors.

For They Know Not What They Do

I watched you digging up the hardened dirt

I watched you placing my passion
down where roots reign

I watched you toss me where the residue
of rainclouds are eventually contained

I watched you pile on top of me opportunities
you thought would stifle me

You see,
as the fear grew inside you,
you placed my seed precisely where
I needed to be

Now I've grown root
Now I've born fruit
Now you are hungry

Should you not then eat where you have labored?

Don't you see?
Even for you,
there is room at my table

*Your inability to reach the depths my treasure is kept
takes no value away from it. Some people dig up dirt
collecting stones, and call them precious.
Other people blast away mountains,
spending days inside them seeking diamonds.
So, you see, I just haven't found the one who truly seeks
what I am.*

It took a while, but I finally understood why canaries don't sing like bluebirds do. So, I flew off into the mist; lost in the bittersweet lullabies of the loneliness that led me to the familiar choir singing inside me.

If you wish to learn something about transformation, it behooves you to pay attention to the caterpillar. For when she is ready to conquer the skies, she cocoons herself away from those trapped where she seeks freedom from.

Language is key in not just identifying things but also in identifying with things. Therefore, you must learn to speak the language of what you seek. Otherwise, you risk the chance of obtaining it, but not being able to truly connect with it.

Ambrosia

I must have lived a few lifetimes before this.
Because this love I carry for you, it induces a sense
of nostalgia for a time and a place I've only seen bits
and pieces of immersed in your soft, unyielding, eyes.
And from listening to the way it speaks of you
with such clarity and wisdom,
I know it is very well acquainted with age.
So, hello, my everlasting.
I am dying to live you, again.

Gift

In the awareness of love,
the eyes lose focus,
purpose,
for that which matters most,
they cannot see

In deep stillness,
as when the night's breeze
forsakes the weeping of the willow's leaves,
her soul,
in silence,
whispered my name in a language
her temporal tongue could not interpret

When nakedness
gave our strange souls
a familiar room to commune,
my spirit shined brighter than a thousand suns
as I lied within her light,
allowing her to witness my shallow
and deeper explorations of her breathing

I can still see clearly in my mind,
our first night beneath the moon's shine
When she placed her mouth against mine,
and my lungs began to malfunction

I have since relived that night
like a recurring dream

Feeling them seeping through recent cracks
of elderly fears, her spoken words
are an orgasmic concoction of divinity
penetrating my wilting aspirations of love

I can still see her soft-textured lips

exploring the rim of my chin
Triggering a deluge of goosebumps
over the entirety of the body
I've concealed myself in

When they departed my skin,
I was left as opened as sacred books bearing
the teachings of ancient things

I can still see the amber light
of the black street lamp partially lighting
her coffee-colored face—casting a silhouette
of beautiful grace against the shadows of egos
that stood between us

I saw that night,
in the brown of her eyes,
intricate patterns of a delicate truth
revealing to me the most arresting prophecy
written of my peace

I read it,
and thus manifested a future seen in the past
into our present space

Now as she rises with each morning,
laying the canopy of her unclothed body
delicately over mine,
syphoning the warmth of my chest,
taking steady breaths as she meditates
upon the future we've conjured together;
I can sense both her familiar
and her unfamiliar selves seeping into my privacy,
eradicating vacancy like the day man slept,
and his God molded Wisdom
from his Innocence

Now,
nightly,

I lie naked in words,
patiently transcribing my desires for her
in every language known to both men
and gods alike as my tongue and my fingers
search the visible her
in the absence of light

Now,
daily,
I watch a falling sun leading a rising moon
in a spellbinding dance across the world
I carry on the inside, just for her

So, I am here in the depths of my musings
Seeking my darling
My soul searching her,
diligently,
thoroughly,
as I watch consciously
our God bringing forth
the very best of me
on the Eve of every good thing
the heavens have conspired
to lay bare before me

For in the awareness of love,
my eyes lost focus,
purpose

For what mattered most,
they could not see

My heart lays a maze of complexities within complexities, but should you endure, my love, you will find all these complexities eventually lead to the simplicity I have found in loving you.

Convergence

Where are you, beloved?
Have you become one with the light of the Sun?
Are you one with his rays of grace?
For in a familiar fashion,
I feel your passion sweeping over me
like untamed fires
as he peruses the honey-like pigment
of your most desired

My Darling,
in him,
as in you,
I have found freedom from my chains,
my fears,
my doubts,
my confined limitlessness

Without hesitation,
he reaches deeply in,
kissing my delicate skin,
familiarly,
unhurriedly

Without hesitation,
I submit to him my everything
I gift to him every sip of my saccharine soul
Familiarly
Hastily

He permeates my material
and my immaterial existence
Navigating my stormy soul with a stillness
your mouth alone have known

His hands bear no resemblance to those
of a stranger

For he touches me with the same breathtaking
patterns you have used to snare
my whimsical heart

Lines traversing my skin
as the many tributaries of a singular river
reveal all the places inside of me
and outside of me
that you have left the tracks
of your irreplaceable love

He traverses them with the grace
of a skilled sailor on a familiar voyage,
but the knowledge of these curves,
I have gifted to you alone

He's played all the chords you've tuned
to perfection within me, darling

He causes me to sing your name
like the lover in fall
awaiting her beloved
in the arms of winter

In meditation,
I inhale the vestiges of the wind
that had their inception in the supernal words
departing your blameless tongue
I can feel them traveling across the open seas
of my flesh, drenched in the sacred waters
you've sprung from my hallowed deep

He's caused my breasts to rise and to fall,
as the cresting and the crashing of the ocean,
in the same fashion you alone have known

Darling, I baptize my sinless nature
in the crystalline waters
of His holy anointing

And so,
you have left me wholly wet,
and yet,
my total self thirsts for all that remains of you

So, tell me, where are you, beloved?
Have you embodied the praise of the Nightingale?
Have you become one with the song sung
within his songs?

Because his melodies echoing
deeply within the expanse of my self
my soul finds as familiar as the divine manner
in which my name sweetly drips
from the blessed tip of your gracious tongue

His song within songs conjures emotions
that translate my ascension into the Highest Self
You are there waiting, yet not waiting
Longing, yet not longing
For where you are, there I always am

We make unblemished love outside
the confines of our limited selves
And when your fire reaches my wick's end,
you lie, still, inside of me
Satiated from untarnished surrender

Darling, my eyes do not contain
the colors of my joy
For my tears reveal the amalgamation
of expressions words have failed
in a thousand attempts to embody

And thus,
all of me in your presence
is present in the lines encasing my lips
as my heart begins to smile
at the sight you

I gaze deeply into the mandalas
of repetitive patterns of love that are your eyes,
and I am one with your soul,
and your soul is one with me,
and we are one with the Highest Self

My Darling,
I've placed my fingers against my own skin,
and felt my heart drumming your name

Her passion as astonishing
as the butterfly's wings
narrating the spirited teachings of the wind

And so, I learn and unlearn all of you
in the divergence of lies and truths
For the singular Truth that you are,
stands an unfaltering champion against
the multitude of Lie and all his versions

So, Darling, I am you
Within you
Waiting, yet not waiting
Longing, yet not longing
For where I am, you always are
For where we are, It always is
The Highest Self

My God
My Self
My Beloved

You are the spark that ignited the fire God has given me for a soul. You speak, and I am engulfed in flames—embers of carnal desires illuminating my outer reaches laid beyond your eyes. Yet, here I am, not consumed.

The Musician and the Muse

Do you know what you are?
You are an acoustic guitar
immaculately explicating
the cavernous musings
of love

And you are the uni-verse song
it keeps rehearsing,
stirring my emotions,
manifesting divine healing
between the fingers of Grace

Do you know what I am?
I am the flickering of the candle's flame
burning in your interlude
Consuming your soul as we took cover
inside your nude
Dancing across the bridge you have erected
between my God and my Self

She came bearing ailments
Past hurts
Unhealed resentments

And then there was my tongue's poetry
Diagnosing and healing the infirmities
of her soul.

Cycles of Devotion

There is a place between her goings
and her comings
It is the place I am most broken

There is a place between her speaking
and her silence
It is where her moon eclipses my sun,
and I gift to her my undivided attention

She is both the chorus and every verse
of my sacred song

A song I've sung in my transitioning
from world to world
Falling apart in love for her
Only to find myself whole again
when she passes her hand against my face
as if to say,
"My Darling, awaken!"

She is the silver chord grounding my soul
to everlasting devotion

The torch burning from my beginning,
guiding my feet,
making certain the uncertainty in each step
as I undergo my mission of finding her again,
every single morning

Honey Making

A flower
She needs not toil
for the honey's maker
to come

In all her radiant beauty,
rooted in the soil of virtue,
she simply stands there,
awaiting him

With a corolla the texture
of wind-swept clouds,
and nectar the flavor
of divinely refined ambrosia,
petals widely open,
she welcomes him

Perhaps she dances a bit
with the unseen wind,
flirting with his attention,
but even this is useless

For each morning,
at the rebirth of the light bringer,
the honey's maker sets out
on his arduous journey,
only to drink of her delightful nature

My silence makes you curious as it rightfully should. Because you haven't seen God as I do when my eyes become full of you.

Therapy

While time sojourned inside our bedroom,
she surveyed the untapped portion of my soul
while the darkness amplified the sound
of 6 a.m. raindrops falling against
freshly laid asphalts

Her naked truth was the color of midair snow,
only a thousand times more pure

I was working
Slowly reacquainting my lips
with the texture of her nakedness
In all the effort, her eyes refused
to divagate from the work of art
I captured her in
As I decorated her celestial mind
with the colors of earthly desires

I inhaled the most intoxicating concoction
of aromas as the air from the ceiling fan fell,
sweeping over her dark and truly lovely

I am no longer to search for love
For the greatest I had ever been,
I found when my mind, my body, and my soul
decided until the heavens fold,
I would exist solely to see the day her eyes
forget what tears ever felt like

In the depths of that night,
as she laid on her back,
eyes slightly tilted towards the complete moon;
I felt her fingers tracing my face with a pace
as though she was trapped
in the same moment of quicksand
that was slowly swallowing the efforts of time

Her arms held the position like one
sacrificing for my transgressions
as she delivered sacred sermons,
hushing unholy exclamations,
exorcising my demons

The darkness of the room held us
like fetuses in the womb

So, I took purpose from my eyes,
embracing my awakening,
as I sniffed from her fragrant skin,
the aroma of body butter

I am so fascinated at how a man can open his mouth, causing a woman to blossom. This is the most beautiful art. How he places words inside of her is beautiful art. For it amplifies the vibrations of her heart, and she, in turn, amplifies those of his.

Daily Bread

I closed my eyes,
distancing myself
from visual distractions
as I bit into the most divinely rich
piece of French pastry
coated with brown sugar
and cinnamon

My God, my Darling,
it reminded me so much
of my daily visits
to your nakedness

She said,
"You feel like home."
Little does she know,
I'd been furnishing my soul for her stay
long before I even knew
her name.

Heart-to-Heart

Where does my strength go
when you come near?
Why do my bones quiver?
Why does my heart race
though my soul be still?
Why are my thoughts many
when my eyes know only you?

Why does my soul find sleep
when you lie with me?
Do I not see more clearly the mercy
God has shown me when I am awake?

Have I lost my wits finding you?
Which side of the night does the day rise?
Where do stars go
when they fall from your eyes?
Is time able to conceive the days and the nights
I have set aside for recounting the journeys
I have traveled within you?

Do you understand that it is my soul
that loves you?

I love your presence because I see God in it
I love your absence because He promised
to come again

Where are the days before you?
Where is the pain that held me captive?

Her tears were the greatest storytellers I'd ever come to know. You should see the way they conveyed the anguish of her caged soul. She was imprisoned yet completely thrilled what I'd perceived to be a free man. I was captivated falling into the depths of her grief, passing brighter days on my way down.

Palace

Inside of me
and inside of you
lies a world
the feet of prior lovers
have not dishonored

In that place,
our minds together is God,
and our thoughts the Spirit's first flight
upon the face of untainted waters

The first night I met you there,
like the moon's reflection upon the face
of midnight oceans,
you allowed your eyes to fall against me
in wonderful curiosity

I saw a softness within you
that was outwardly divine

I felt my hands slowing your breathing
as you submitted,
and I imparted my fingers' prints
over the entirety of the scene

Because in here, darling,
it is a crime to pass away from your world
until I have explored every single inch of you

When you stepped into my presence,
I heard the cries of wind and stringed
instruments

I looked
I noticed the trees no longer swayed
The birds no longer sang

And the clouds no longer moved
beneath the brightly blue sky

For the wind became obsessed,
losing itself in your garments
And the birds altogether
could not compose a tune
as tranquil as the sound of the words
departing your mouth

In a jealous rage,
the clouds dissipated
from the skies above

Because in all their efforts,
they could not reflect
the glory of the sun
quite the way that you do

Darling, I see you
But you've constructed fortresses of fear
Cementing behind memories of failed endeavors,
the desires of God that burn within you

But darling,
in the absence of oxygen,
the consuming flame becomes but a flicker

And in time,
and unless you allow me to breathe into you,
the darkness will subdue your fire, too

But if my light guides your feet,
and if your light guides my feet,
our dance will never lead us into the shadows
where traps lie for those who are hopeless
for each other

I once dreaded the thought of the last breath

escaping the snare I've set in my lips

But Darling, this is death
To not have my light inside your light
To not have your light inside my light
To not find your self inside my self
To not perceive my soul inside your own

For from the lips of the Anointed it was spoken,
let them be in me
as I AM
in you

This is the realization of God
To love your soul as I do my own

And this is the realization of God
To bestow the highest praise upon the One
who considered the dust I've shrouded myself in
worthy to walk upon the polished floor
of the palace
that you are

Permit me stay between your lips, and I'll prove to you the soul has no need for the waste of trees.

Bloom

My Flower sat amidst spring's blossoms
Orange-yellows like Caribbean suns
setting in mid-September

Purples adorning sage petals
like garments fit for royal women

I read the brown of her eyes
like sacred poetry

Enchanted by her aroma
A Blue Monarch butterfly navigating
the gold-washed serpent-like strands
of unrestrained hair

Plum-colored lips
I slow-sipped of her silence
My fingers smearing the essentials
of Jasmine over her cocoa skin

My Flower blossomed at the tip
of my fertile touch
Whispers of my heart
watering withered aspirations

She opened up

*When I met you,
I chose you,
consciously.
I have chosen you
every single day since,
consciously.*

Holy Ground

My most beloved,
I marvel at the construction of your temple

Finely architected and layered
in unearthly colors,
you reveal the most exquisite details
of heavenly places my sublunary eyes
have ever witnessed

You are
my place
of worship

And so, as I submit supplications
between your inward and your outward selves,
perusing the perfect symmetry between your soul
and your unclothed body,
it is quite evident your Creator
was well versed in the understandings
of sacred geometry

Beloved, you are fine art in all the intricacies
of all your dimensions

So, I surrender my sinful nature
at the center of your most holy
Reciting like a mantra the sacred sounds
rising from your crested soul
as I gracefully make divine love to it

And like a chakra,
I rose from your lowest self
to your highest self
And when the singular point
of enlightenment had fully come,
we ascended when with understanding

I placed my lips between your eyes
Witnessing the passing of the man I knew
before the day the universe conspired
for me to find you

My darling,
the birthing of the lightning
was our souls forsaking the orbit of God
as we descended into the realm of flesh,
beneath the watchful eyes of darkness

My love,
you are the embodiment of Love
And thus, I prostrate myself before you
Ascribing devotion as both my lips
and my tongue rehearse the notes
that gave cadence to the saccharine song
I composed from the muffled sounds
rising from your satisfaction

And at night,
as you make sweet love to me,
I adorn your nakedness with poetry
far exceeding the mastery
of Michelangelo's artistry

And so, my air,
I lie often in the silence of you
My lips immersed in the gentle flow of you
Ingesting life, dining on the fruit of you
Learning the secrets of your garden
that compelled me to fall, for you

Watchman

There is a night, my Love,
that sits in the most terrifying depths of my mind

If courage should persuade you,
it is the darkest you shall ever see
But when you've arrived,
do not permit fear the use of your heart

Because its crescent moon
lying in the nude
amidst a cluster of stars
is but a reflection
of the Light of God abiding within you

Its pillars of flaming fire
are the answered prayers
I have carried within my soul,
just for you

If you wish to manifest us,
allow your heart to walk boldly,
disrobed of anticipated outcomes,
and come I will to you

From the morning I looked within myself,
and saw the soul guised in flesh
staring in the reflection of the water
that lies at the feet of the heavens,
I have meditated on the wisdom of God
How He carefully placed these prayers
scattered over the night's sky,
solely for your heart to make wishes upon me

So, go, my Darling
Lie down
Find your rightful place out where dreams

run unchained

Offer yourself
Allow the bed I have finessed
from my musings of you
to take you places in my stead

But tell him,
if you will,
I beg of him,
to never dishonor your submission

Tell him neither his eyes nor his hands
should ever be found away from you

And should you rise ahead of the sun,
drenched in the residue of wonderful dreams,
know that I came to you,
knowing every inch of you,
beneath the naked skies
where I lie scattered,
keeping vigil
over you

Reflecting Pool

My otherwise tumultuous soul is perfectly still

Cherry blossoms are quietly revealing
the hiding places of the child-like wind

Pink and white pieces of Heaven
falling like sanctified souls
at the culmination of earthly purpose

They fall against a collection of leaves
bearing various shades of green,
and a patchwork of white clouds
partially veiling an irresistibly blue sky

A flawless picture framed inside
a picturesque lake sleeping in perfected peace

Off in the near distance
sits a wearied man
well acquainted with the glory of age

His wrinkled hands playing upon piano keys
like spirited children in piles of autumn's leaves

Darling, all of this beauty, this poetry,
has given me one revelation

God is still trying to do again
what He's already done
inside of you

Our sin came like a spring of water.
Our best attempt at dowsing the fire we lit together.
But our souls were lustfully entanglement
in a conversation sparked between our silence.
And so, we burned.

And so, we burned.

Mirage

Shapeless, and without color

I am as water whenever
I find myself inside of you
Allowing thoughts of you
pooled inside of me
to mimic the seraphic patterns
that give form to the eternal you

Your perceptions of my colors
are but reflections of you
A beauty I have only been able to reflect
through the labor of the pen
as my heart breaks and mends
in a perpetual fashion
as it makes room for more of you

Sweetheart,
all that is seen inside of me
is but the refraction of the light that is you
How you penetrate the depths of my distraction
while I drown in the shallows of you

*She comes to me in phases.
Sometimes like a deluge, other times just a slight trickle.
Something like night rain over Miami.*

Rain Dance

I fall having no agendas
Yet I know some,
like children,
will dance beneath the open skies
while others will open umbrellas

You see, My Love, my love has no versions

It is how you receive me
that will decide
whether your feet
will have you
dancing in my downpour
or running for barren places

Still, here I am
Pouring from all that I am
Waiting to wash you in a love
that will never permit your skin
to flake in the anger of the sun

Replenished

Her tears flow from the river of God
I am no fool

I place parched lips eagerly beneath her eyes
each time she cries
I am no fool

Every time I've ever left something of my heart on a blank sheet of paper, I've learned that I have loved you in ways and in places I was not yet mindful of.

Song of Her King

I adore the ways and the places
in which you kiss me

Because of you,
my soul dances on the other side of my flesh
whenever it is, and wherever it is
your lips fall against me

You,
my most loved,
are exceedingly more breathtaking
than the rising moon bathing
in the river of fire cascading
from the dying sun

Thus,
I sing from my inner-self praises to you
as the Wolf serenading his luminous moon
in the midst of a glorious night

Darling,
when yesterday was conceived,
I was the lifeless remains of the valley
a mighty river had forsaken

Dried bones were my inheritance
after the feasting of famished vultures

But today,
with the coming of you,
I am the summit of an erected mountain
bathing in the residue of your passing through

My Love, when the sun fell,
and the night-sky gifted us privacy,
in my eyes your motions were seamless

as I followed the periphery of your nakedness

I saw the piercing eye of the complete moon
sneaking through a crack in the window
Lighting just enough of your skin
to impart a deeper appreciation
for the mastery of God

You satisfied my desires of flesh
as I journeyed through your wetlands
Lips saturated in your unhindered truth

I was without life, yet completely living
I was without words, yet fluently speaking

Because you,
in my arms,
at night,
and when the world goes silent,
is the restorative work of God
making old things anew

And for this,
and for you,
my total self gives untainted praise

In Her Garden

Amidst a scenic sea of green,
you are the red wildflower
beguiling my wandering eyes

*From the dark of her ash,
a crimson Rose grew.*

Resurrecting Love

In the time of my winter,
she interrupted my season
like the birthing
of spring

What things I perceived as dead
she brought to life again
Enlightening me on the perpetual nature
of the soul
Hers having been born many times
in many worlds

She sprung from my infertile mind
like a child conceived in infertile time

She made me to understand
that death and life are the left
and right hands of God
Cycling through my transience
like a seasoned potter remastering
the blemishes of his masterpiece

And so, she goes
And so, she comes
God, in her many manifestations
Never forgetting when
I need Her most

Somewhere between the watchful moon, an endless sea of prying stars, and the serenade of journeyed waves upon the yearning sand, God breathed against my soul when she placed her lips gently between my helpless eyes.

Guardians of Her Soul

He found his place in the space between her eyes
and the steady heavy melancholic melody
of a guitar conjuring his jealousy

The sun was descending,
gasping for life,
gifting his moon his last ray of light

He crowned her life
as the light that crowns the head
of one walking amongst the dead

Snatching him up from the flesh,
he was in the midst of her heaven

Feeling her divine pulse coursing
through his immaterial existence

Entrenched deeply beyond the surface
of honey-brown patterns of pretty,
he sat quietly,
unraveling her mystery

Her eyes perfectly placed erased doubt
Casting fears from his inner place

And certainly,
he was lost in the place
all the colors converge,
having never been inside her darkness before

But all of her felt amazingly familiar

She became to him the door
which leads the weary home
having journeyed countless days

in stranger places

Her consternation beguiled his eyes
like midnight constellations

Even the shadows casted
beneath her dejected eyes
were enough light to guide his heart
through the darkness that stood inside
and outside of her

Morning's Brew

With a complexion reminiscent
of roasted coffee beans
bathing beneath
golden streams
of the Jamaican sun,
each morning,
I rise to divinely brewed
doses of your delicacy

Cello's Lament

I sat once in the holy worship
of a lamenting Cello

She wept for the loss of her beloved

O, how she poured out her soul before me

I have since tried finding the words
to convey what I felt inside,
but failure has greeted me along the way
as the morning's light
greets the night's glory
at the commencement
of the new day

You were there,
sitting in the place I have kept vacant
for God's most precious

She offered to us the blessings of Love
We accepted

We worshipped in the beauty of holiness
Your uncovered breasts
against my uncovered chest
in the depths of a Cello's lament

We were a symphony
The envy of all things holy

A masterfully composed song,
bellowing from the mouth of God

I thought to make corrections in the direction we chose to the well that is now empty. But as my beloved and I sat at the place no water was to quench our thirst, I realized, having searched the depths of her eyes, that all along the thirst I sought to quench was her.

Raunclouds and Sunflowers

I once heard a sunflower weeping
in the wake of rainclouds
It was a Sunday morning
And about as gloomy as any lonely heart
could ever be

She was broken beautifully
And just as amazing
Serenading my pain as if I was something
she could possibly feel

And though I couldn't move,
I danced with every word
that escaped her crippling circumstance

I had never heard sadness more arresting
come from the lips of anything

I was caught up in a whirlwind
of repressed emotions
Wanting to comfort her breaking heart,
but her discomfort was, in fact, my healing

I thought of the house she would find her place
and the home she would someday put together
It made me deeply envious
Because her pieces were coming together,
and they were absolutely breathtaking

Somewhere beneath these skies, my beloved wanders in search of her beloved, and thus, my heart leaps within as a lighthearted calf playing in the morning's rain.

Alchemy

Somewhere, between her brilliant eyes
and beautiful insignificance,
in the restraints of words
that made bare unsullied intentions,
I found myself with life
and breathing where death permits
no other such privilege

Such beautiful alchemy

I go where she is the very best of me
In flesh
In submissiveness
In fearlessness
I go

I come back—always—
bearing only that of myself
death possesses no privilege to possess

And whenever I become weary,
and when the world that I carry
begins to leave scars on arching my shoulders,
she allows me graciously
to sit quietly between the verses
of her composition
For there is healing in her transcendent song
And restoration in the melody
that she carries for a soul

Such beautiful alchemy

This melody is far more consoling
than any whisper aging leaves
and transient breeze could ever gather

Over me, she has carful dominion
My Melody abiding outside the restraints
of quiet interlude

I am never both alone with her
and naked of unveiled attention
She holds compassion like oceans do
raging waters
And like rivers, I run hastily to her
Emptying my burdens inside an embrace
more calming than the somnolent eyes
of the newly born

You see, I have been everywhere, though nowhere
I have seen everything, though blindly
I have held malicious intentions
against my unclothed skin
wherever lust led my discontented soul

But until just now
Until we spoke without the measure of words
Until our emptied bodies lied like open coffins
where a silvery moon kisses the charcoal ocean

Until the ocean
—satiated by midnight's silence—
baptized our bared bodies like sinners
in the company of conceding divinity
Have I realized that the soul's mate
is not merely the soul of another

For this melody, she is my soul
She is my freedom framed in a window
I'd yet possessed the privilege to open

This melody has changed me

Such beautiful alchemy

Sweet Spell

When the Honeybee
alights himself upon the face of his flower,
he flies away—always—gleefully
Her sweet spell dispersed all over him

Being a scholar, I spread her mind apart studying the fine art of deep penetration.

God in Her Flesh

With a mind as immense
as the universe's dream
and ever expanding

In vivacious colors
completely pale
in her comparison

Words sprung from the dearth of my emotions
like wildflowers breaking barren soil
when the rains finally come

I decorated the canvas-like soul of my beloved,
then hung her in repeated patterns
on the interminable walls of my time

Gazing into the distance
where stars are conceived,
I sought the beginning
of that which encompasses everything

But when my search left me
as filled as the well
waiting in the place
clouds have forsaken,
I searched the butterflies'
dancing with the unseen wind
in the passing of midday rain

I searched the remains of stars falling from time
like a woman with fruit
miscarrying her light

I searched the song the bluebird sang
when the rising sun drew the morning's dew
from her wings

I searched the depths
of the piano's pain
when masterful fingers
stroked her in all the right places

I searched

I searched the variance of the colors
adorning my aging skin

I searched Mona Lisa's impeccable smile,
and the brilliant mystery
of Starry Night's brush strokes

But my search left me as filled
as a well waiting in the place
clouds have forsaken

Then I searched the smile of my darling

I searched the patterns
etched into the brown of her eyes

I searched the search of her eyes
passing between my lips
and my eyes

I searched the breaths she refused to take
as I inhaled her as though death was clawing
at my material self

I searched the undulation of her hair
dancing in the subtle wind
that snuck too closely against her skin

I searched the grace of her steps
and the singular dimple just to the left
of the most satisfying lips I have ever drank of

I searched the words she spoke

into my wilted dreams
like the evening rain rejuvenating wilting leaves

Then I searched the way she danced
to the piano's concerto

How she moved with time and rhythm
as though neither of them existed

And there
Right there where my life was hanging
in a solitary moment

Right there where every possible need
became all that she ever was

It was there,
where her music took me places I haven't been,
that God permitted me to see how glorious
She truly is

Awhile

Rest awhile
Let me remove those burdens
from your journeyed feet

Just sit with me
Awhile

Dance awhile
Let us lose our way in the path
this piano is paving

Close your eyes
You won't need them

Just follow me
Awhile

Lie down awhile
Let us watch the sun's light
playing with the morning's wind
between see-through curtains

Maybe then you will understand
what it is my heart feels when it is dancing
with the veil of your innocence

Darling, rest awhile
Let me remove those worries
from your beautiful mind

Just be still
Just be mine
Just inhale me

Awhile

Whenever we kiss, everything beautiful in the deep of your soul surfaces in the shallow of your eyes.

Headdress

You exist amidst the brightest colors
of a divine flame

I conjure you into the late of night
Lighted candles casting the shadows
of your dimensions against my vacant soul

You surround me on every side,
emitting the aroma of Magnolia
and White Gardenia

How you captivate the eye of my understanding

Dancing in the air of my presence
like torn pages of sacred scripture
tossed in a steady wind

You are a holy thing from worlds unknown
enthroned just beyond my bounds of fear

You are a deluge of untainted water
sprung from the tongue of our Creator

I immerse my total self within yours
Suspended between your impeccable
appearance, and the ambient sounds
of wind instruments rising
from the depths of your inner being

You are the mounted headdress of a wise King

Bearing a scepter of compassion,
your King rules from a place
of unblemished understanding,
for you stand the storehouse of his wisdom

Far more mystical than the wind,
you go and you come again
without regard to expectations

Whenever you steal away from the heavens,
I am ever pleased,
and never ashamed
Though I stand before you unveiled of secrets

You are the most persistent,
most consistent, reminder
that my God's love
is ever present

Stargazing

I lied with the nakedness of the earth
Watching the aging sun
clothing everything breathtaking
as it fell from the crest of heaven

I saw how a cotton field of cumulous clouds
transfigured from the essence of snow
to an intoxicating concoction
of a rainbow's residue

I watched until the darkness was perfect
Something like the smile that resided
upon the lips of my beloved

I wrapped my arms around her
Something like the way the sunless heavens
cuddled the souls of distant stars

That night, she became the light
that had never lit my soul
She became the place silence was flawless
And I became deaf to the sounds
of bitter jealousy as envious stars wept over us

My eyes were completely full of her
My darkness receded in shame

That night,
lying with her earth,
she fell with beauty over my nakedness,
clothing shameful insecurities,
sort of like the sun,
only not aging the same

Arise

Awaken, my love
My light resides in your eyes
My darkness has fully come
And there is no fear like that of loving someone
that isn't you

Won't you take my breath far away
—again—
like rising suns and dying suns used to do
before the perfect day that I met you?

Awaken, my love
Set your eyes again to the pathway of my soul
For the place its God sits has become vacant

Rise in peace, my love
For you are the pulse that sends life
coursing through my dying truth

My heart's beat, arise from your sleep
For the hour of our ascension has come

Arise, my love
Have your place among the stay of burning stars
For I burn for you as they do
You that sparked from the conflagration
of our God

You,
my love,
are my life

So, arise

*It quenches the thirst of the passerby, yet the well itself takes
not a sip of its water.
I am your servant.*

I Drink of You

I drink of you, my love

Like the deer thirsting for more of life,
feet planted in the gentle flow
of the quiet water brook,
places his lips in its life-giving nature,
taking sips of the water's kindness

So, too, I plant my soul in the gentle flow
of your solitude

And when the sacredness of all that you are
manifests in your flesh,
I take sips of your selflessness

I drink of you, my love

A flawless seed will fail to bear fruit if not sown, watered, and cared for. So, if you wish for her to bear fruit in your future, sow her diligently in your presence. Then water her with gratitude each day, and never forget to cover her skin with the gentlest kisses between the falling of the sun and the rising of the moon.

Gardener

The Gardener cultivated a garden of one flower

With his own hands,
he expressed a love as pure
as the words from God's mouth
that called forth the first moon

From his soul,
he spoke life over her barren womb

Then he placed his fingers
—with great patience—
into the dark of her soil
Making room
for the love seed
she awaited to bloom

She conceived!
His flower conceived!

She was the delight of all that he was,
and everything that he was not

The aromatic amalgam
of Sweet Autumn Clematis,
Stargazer Lily,
Honeysuckle,
and Jasmine

Voice of Silence

You wonder why I find so much comfort
in silence

If only you knew
the conversations I carry with you
when my lips become silent

Darling, there aren't words bold enough
to stand up to the sentiments I carry you in

Sometimes I think to speak,
but then your eyes hold me and I get so weak

You wonder do I love you enough
If only you knew I only take air into my lungs
to prolong my stay at your side

You should know that if death
came for me this night
and you weren't around
I'd give him no fight

You should know those quiet nights
—when I do not speak—
I am actually searching the depths of you,
discovering new ways of seeing you

My love, I will search a thousand worlds
—a thousand different lifetimes—
until I've shown your soul
—a thousand different ways—
that you are more to me
than the air that I breathe
Even when I am here
Deep in the silence

I must ask your absolution ahead of what's to come. You will feel a slight sensation as though I am trying to eat your soul. I am.

Healer

The sound of your name
passing between my lips
is the envy of a thousand
stringed instruments
having a singular vibration

It is a river's flow birthed in the cleft
of a rock struck by divine wisdom

I drank thereof
I am renewed

When I doubted the existence of God,
you opened your heart
You gave me revelation

As a child endeavored to ensnare the wind
in a basket composed purely of aging straws,
I sought to take possession of you,
and so learned my ignorance
was the greater master

You are the healing room of my restoration

You are a great book
opened in the hands of God,
and inscribed with divine psalms
that anointed my shortcomings
like oil blessed by the sacred chants
of a thousand holy men

You beheld the residue of what I once was
Unlived-in ambitions decaying on the pile
of forgotten dreams

The tainted pieces of my former self,

like blood-bought silver,
failed to redeem my wretched ways

But you kept mercy
But you healed me

You recited my name,
and awoken my slumbering soul
in a language spoken from the sanctified lips
of Love

Your broken flesh interceding for my sinful ways
was my altar of salvation

You passed your hands in the gentlest motion
against my uncomely face

I closed my eyes to find the Light of God
inside of you,
and every perfect reason
to remain there

I lived, and I died that very instant
I lived, and I died that very instant
I lived, and I died, that very instant

But you kept mercy

Addiction

In my search for you,
I was told to keep my heart
from such futile endeavor
For love isn't a thing you find
but a realization you surrender to

Do you have any idea what it is I feel
that compels me to gaze so easily
—so mindlessly—
into the realm of your eyes?

Like jazz instrumentals
domesticating untamed emotions,
out where the moon reigns supreme,
and the conversation is soul-deep,
your eyes, they sooth where all else have failed

I often go off into your imaginations
And I sit to witness your heart creating worlds
the feet of lustful men have never defiled

When I am there, I am in the company of words
so pure the tongues of idle men are forbidden
to make mention of them

You rest your lips upon mine, Darling,
and my soul is a raging fire
Yet somehow you remain as cool
as southern wind in late December

My love, like the sweetest addiction,
you are something to be experienced
a few times over

Even if it be that you should be the end of me

The books of spiritual things teach that God called the void into existence. I was dancing with my doubts, until I saw what your lips did with the mess that you met me in.

Memoirs of Her King

There is a garden of scented flowers
where my barren heart used to be
Whenever he exposes his soul,
whether in or out of season,
I blossom

Both his tongue and his fingers
are masterful poets
I am their muse
My body I lay quietly before them
My soul always in the nude

He writes sonnets of the glister in my eyes,
and the starry heavens recede in shame
Each night I empty his cup,
but he is replenished again before the rising sun
breaks the yielding horizon

Each morning, with patience I can only imagine,
he gives to me of the newness he receives
Leaving evidence of his essence
as he passes through my sacred entrance

He is my King,
my counselor,
my teacher,
my lover

He carries me off into the unending field
of dreams his God has concealed
beneath those winsome eyes

Out there, I sit in deep meditation,
allowing his heart's beat to sound my mantra,
and so bear witness to the Seven Spirits of Love
rising in perpetual patterns from the thoughts

he's kept only for me
Each time he comes to me,
without disappointment,
he places his strong arm in the arch
of my lower back,
and I submit without hesitation

Moving consciously into him
like a disembodied soul
into the arms of redemption

When he kisses me,
between the moment he rests his lips
between my eyes, and the moment
he takes them away,
I know the beginning and the ending
of ten thousand lives
Yet his skin remains as refined as the day
his God fashioned him

In times past, he found me drifting
Lifelessly drifting in my river that raged
Hurts and resentments
Pain and sadness
Defeat had seeped so deep into my lungs
I lost both the desire, and the ability to breathe

But seeing the flicker of flame
that was fading inside of me,
My King swam courageously
into the raging madness that held me bound

He pulled me from the place I was left to take
the last breath I was clinging to

He placed his mouth upon me,
and freely recited poetry he hadn't yet written

From the unforgiving darkness,

I heard every word that broke the lips
of the love that resurrected me

And so,
I carry a garden of sweet-scented flowers
where my barren heart used to be

Now,
be it in season
or out of season,
I blossom each time he exposes his soul

Stranger in Her Skin

How do you manage, Darling
Having spent all of your life
inside your own skin,
and still having no idea
how delightful it truly is
against the tongue?

Reflection

He read a thousand questions in her eyes,
but only one fell to her lips

"Why did you choose me?"
"I was selfish," he said

"I'd been trying to find the best version
of myself"
"Turned out all this time, I was right here inside
of you"

Her eyes are a place sanctified.
With the rise of each morning, I enter in, shedding my sin.
Inside there, I have no need of air; for she is life,
every place I turn about inside of her.
It saddens me each time my atonement is complete,
though I only leave to dirty myself again.

Morning's Meditation

To breathe is to love you

To think is to realize dreams of you,
and you are every single reason
that makes me desire the land of the living

I am thankful every single morning
that I still have eyes to see
those beautiful creases in your cheeks

They embellish your smile
in ways you cannot fathom

I adore the way the morning's sun lies quietly
against your face

Entranced,
it incites a tinge of jealousy in my eyes,
but who am I to rob myself of the art
no finger has created?

I am certain God is searching
for His Crown Jewel
the way the sun looks down on you

The perfect balance of sleeping,
and awakening caught in your partially
opened eyes

My perfect reflection safely inside them

I am deathly in love with you, Darling
Yet reluctant to touch your skin
Can you imagine I move even a single strand
of hair out of place?

I love everything about you
just the way you are
right this very second

And when tomorrow comes,
I will fall again for everything you are today,
only your head won't lie against the pillow
exactly the same way

What mean I of this?
I mean that I love every single second
of your beautiful transition

All my days I have wandered in lust,
amusing transient feelings,
trying to find my higher self
in lower things

But eyes upon you,
I heard with my own heart
the words God spoke
the morning he mastered His art,
"She, is very good"

I, give praise

If you think the one placing their lips against your skin is something, wait until you meet the one who places them against your soul.

It Is Really You

I love the place you keep me inside your eyes

I wish to breathe when I'm there,
but breaths take time,
and forever is no possession of mine

I'd imagined difficulty loving you
outside of that place
and so I ran,
far away,
but I came home,
and not a single second had past

To love you forever is all that I need

Before we kissed,
or I felt the texture of your words
as they paralyzed my thinking,
you were my darling

Now time is eroding my sanity,
and there is a fire inside of me that burns
to the jealousy of hell each time I think
our earthly stay will someday end

I have asked God questions I could
no longer keep secret,
but you are still a secret

My best kept

It is really you
My soul's mate

Heart Song

You are somewhere
between the harmonious play
of the grand piano battling silence,
and the crackling sound of light embers
echoing inside fireplaces

I sometimes fight the universal will
Still you manage to pull me in
as I rehearse you again and again

You are the first
and the last melody
my heart has truly ever sung

With each rise of the sun,
I become enslaved to the will of my pen
Blessing these empty pages
Writing incoherent phrases
This most futile effort of the ages
Trying to compose you all over again

I Search for You

In days of perpetual lonesomeness,
drenched in undignified desire,
I search for you

Remembering the sadness
that greeted me in your eyes,
becoming the jester that gives birth
to that gorgeous smile,
I search for you

Out where the birds sing
to your dispirited heart,
reciting the words to your song,
I search for you

Remembering the love I felt in our past,
shivering with fear outside your presence,
I search for you

If you adore the sound of the breeze making its way through the trees, do not try to silence it. If you are in awe of the sea's wave crashing against the sand, do not try to bottle it. If you love the freedom that draws you to a woman, do not try to chain her hands. To truly love something is to love the very essence of its untamed ways. Any attempt to alter, possess, or tame it, for personal gratification, is the paragon of selfishness, and selfishness is a contaminant of love.

You're Not That Amazing

Akin waterfalls playing silent stones
like tribal drums for the attending wind,
on a mild Sunday morning,
your face,
by itself,
is a
poem

Eurhythmic
Spiritual
Wonderful

And whenever it is,
or wherever it is
that you come piercing through
my cluttered thoughts like midday suns
through sycamore branches,
I devote time, etching your smile
into the deep of my mind
Studying its features as zealous men do
the sacred texts of earthly religions

In the attendance of your soul,
I see a conciliating congregation
of Caribbean palm trees,
white sandy beaches,
vibrantly colored clouds
reluctantly passing on unhurried winds,
and the dimmed light of Aruban sunsets
reflected on turquoise seas

The expanse of your legs is a journey
I purposely lose my way in
And each time that I reach the sanctuary
at which they end,
I've discovered expressions of love I had yet

given the freedom to flee the confines
of my tongue

My darling,
I could compose books of riveting prose
just recounting the things I feel
engaging my soul against your skin

Your hands, they are masters at spell-casting

And I have watched night after night
how your faithful fingers have done
their bidding, refacing my blemished heart
as they pull my fractured self beneath
the fountain of healing
you keep between your lips

Darling, to speak of your eyes is to disclose
the obsolescence of oxygen

And I swear the God of Heaven
passes through my earth each time
that you lie in my arms naked of inhibitions

Whenever it is that you smile,
I can feel something of the divine pulling
at my laden soul

Even the varied shades of brown
adorning your covering leave my fingers
exploring as I count, for me,
the many blessings that you have been

I watch loose strands of your golden hair,
like spirited children,
playing hide and seek with the unseen wind,
and feel God in all its glory

My love, Do you know how much I adore

going inside of you?
Being deeply submerged until every ounce
of all that I am is felt in the core that exudes
the beautiful miracle that bears your name?

Now darling,
I know there are many that often fall victim
to the captivating spell that you call a body

And though I may be the first
and the last of them
—still—
it is the art that you are on the inside
that I have chosen to hang on the wall
my heart has kept vacant for God's
magnum opus

But listen, my sweet Darling,
you are really not that amazing

In the Cool of Every Day

I thirst for you, my love
To lay my body in the cool of the shadow
you cast between my darkness
and your light

To lose my way in the way of your eyes
For they carry all captives to your soul

To sit at the mercy of the wind teasing
with doses of the aromas leaving your quietude

To place my lips against yours,
and drink of the reservoir of life God
has hidden within your silence

Each time my existence senses your existence,
I lose total control of my total self

When I came into possession
of the knowledge that the love I needed was you,
you were lying on the caramel-colored couch
reciting the lines of poetry
between my soul
and my body

I watched the steady rising and falling
of your chest as you took breaths of God's
magnificence into you

I took notice of the lines
in the canary-yellow summer's dress
as it mimicked your enticing curves
to the rise of my curiosity

Your fingers, with divine patience,
flipped through my book,

and I was enamored by the way your eyes
glanced over my skin as your mouth
—in silence—
revealed the uncharted depths beyond my eyes

My love,
there isn't a night our earth has seen
that I do not give praise to our God
for His kindness found within you

My love,
I have learned this,
and it has blessed me immensely

I am you,
and you are me,
and we exist in the place
God comes among us
in the cool of every day

And for this, I give praise

Between the Heavens and Myself

Why do you permit them to pollute the voice
of reason that echoes inside your clarity?

Listen!
Do you not hear my fervent intercessions for you?
They say you aren't that beautiful
as though a rose with broken petals
doesn't melt the hearts of the truly conscious

Look!
Do you not see that I am caught in the air
of you?
They say you aren't worth my time,
because they weren't there when God gifted
His essence and wrapped His truth
like a bow around you

My love, you are that place between the heavens
and myself

The place my prayers dwell

Darling, you are a song to me
So beautiful
So peaceful
So true

Do you not see how the skies have become
my playground?
And what difference there lies between your eyes
and the skies?
Are they both not the habitation of our God?
Do you not believe that I give praise for you?

Just ask the days that have seen us together,
and see which among them is the liar

Sacred Seed

They will not understand
They will see,
but blindness will rule them
They will hear,
but our interpretation will elude them
They will feel, but their hearts,
in a thousand lifetimes,
will never permit them the courage to endure us

My divine permitted me to dine on her glory
I was perfectly broken,
and drinking of her provision
like sinners partaking of holy communion

In the temporal position—as one praying—
I saw God, her sanctified self,
and all that she drew from me

I wish to all that lives that I could convey
to you the colors of her soul,
but the rainbow has not been so blessed

I wish to all that lives that I could share
with you the immensity of her love,
but there isn't a snare in this world
to remove God from his rest

So, you will look with your eyes,
but blindness shall beset you
And you will listen with your ears,
but our language shall defy you
And you will feel with the entirety
of your heart, but in all your cycles of life,
you shall not possess the capacity
to endure the gravity of what
my most beloved carries on the inside, just for me

Wind Chimes

At night,
when the darkness leaves me open,
she passes through my mind
like a timorous gust of wind

Allowing me to sing more delicately
than wind chimes

I keep nothing away from her

She knows my insanity
Loving her through all the cycles of myself
Scripting her in the poetry
my lips shall never recite

At night,
when the darkness leaves me open,
she passes through my mind
like a timorous gust of wind,

Allowing me to sing more beautifully
than wind chimes

Benediction

You loved me with a tangible boldness,
but it was the subtle moments
of well-intentioned affection
—endearing thoughts possessing
fingers that knew the places
my fears I kept—
that kept me tethered to your world

I was never whole
But your tongue was kind words,
sublime grace,
and a silence my noise grew to crave

Your heart was as pure as the eyes
you saw me through
But, to you, I was only confusion
An amalgam of stupid expressions
too naïve to receive its final benediction

I drew your pain so much
I learned to call it by name

You did not deserve that
And I did not deserve you

I am nothing left outside the inadequacy
that I am to you this day

You deserved to walk away
But I am grateful that you chose to stay

You have gifted me days inside a world
I couldn't otherwise perceive

I go with the sun, always, ahead of me
The moon, always, keeping the shadows

at bay behind

In time, I will surrender, my all, to time
And what memories of me you keep
will be my last benediction

Those subtle moments
of well-intentioned connection—
keeping me tethered to your world

C.L. Brown was born and raised on the island of Jamaica. He immigrated to the United States at age eleven. As conveyed in his work, Brown is profoundly inspired by the very essence of life. His work has garnered him much acclaim for his poetic style and accent-rich delivery. In the words of American actress, Kimberly Elise, Brown is "changing the world one brilliant and authentic poetic word at a time."

He's authored several poetry collections including *Bare, and Loud Whispers of Silent Souls*. Residing in Miami, Brown enjoys gardening and spending time with his life partner and daughter, Luna Marverly.

www.ingramcontent.com/pod-product-compliance
Lightning Source LLC
Chambersburg PA
CBHW060559080526
44585CB00013B/624